SMART DIY: BOOK II

The Ground-Up Compromise:

Why Smart DIYers Let Pros Handle the Foundation Before Picking Up a Hammer

Smart DIY - Volume II

Written by Thomas Quirk
Edited by Angélica Díaz
Review and Design by Angélica Díaz

First Edition: 2026
Production:

SMART DIY: BOOK II

The Ground-Up Compromise:

Why Smart DIYers Let Pros Handle the Foundation Before Picking Up a Hammer

CONTENT

INTRODUCTION

THE DESIGN-DRIVEN ADVANTAGE

The dream of building an Accessory Dwelling Unit (ADU) in Southern California is often overshadowed by the reality of its cost. The price tag for a fully finished, contractor-built ADU can easily soar past $300,000, making the return on investment questionable for many homeowners. This book presents a powerful alternative: the Design-Driven DIY ADU. This model is not about doing everything yourself; it is about strategically investing in professional design, engineering, and permitting services upfront so that the construction phase is simplified, de-risked, and ready for the owner-builder to execute.

In this model, the professional team—the architect, the engineer, and the permit expediter—effectively acts as your general contractor on paper. They provide you with a set of fully vetted, code-compliant, and highly detailed plans that minimize the guesswork and the potential for costly errors during the build. This strategic investment in planning allows you to bypass the high fees of a General Contractor (GC), saving you tens of thousands of dollars, while still ensuring the structural integrity and legality of your project.

Ultimately, this guide is about understanding the system well

The key difference between this approach and a typical "Hybrid" build (where a GC handles the structural shell) is that here, you, the homeowner, manage the entire construction process, from site prep to final finish. However, you do so with the confidence of a professional blueprint. This trade-off—more upfront design cost for massive construction savings—is the smartest path for the hands-on homeowner who wants maximum control over their budget and timeline. This guide will walk you through every step, from defining your vision to obtaining your final Certificate of Occupancy.

PART I

THE PROFESSIONAL FOUNDATION (DESIGN & ENGINEERING)

CHAPTER 1

DEFINING YOUR ADU VISION

After working with hundreds of ADU homeowners and reviewing countless projects that went over budget or stalled in redesign, one pattern shows up every time: **the projects that succeed start with a clear, written vision.**

Before you hire an architect, talk to an engineer, or think about construction timelines, there is one essential step you must take:

> *Decide exactly what your ADU is meant to do..*

This may sound obvious, but it is one of the most important decisions in your entire ADU project. A clearly defined vision keeps your design focused, prevents expensive changes later, and ensures that the money you spend on plans and permits is used wisely. When your goal is clear from the beginning, everything that follows—design, approvals, and construction—moves faster and more smoothly.

Function Comes First: Let The Purpose Guide the Design

The way you plan to use your ADU will directly determine its size, layout, features, and even construction cost. Start by identifying its primary purpose. Everything else flows from this decision.

Design professionals consistently agree on this point: when function is unclear, costs rise, and plans change.

Option 1: Rental Income

If your ADU is meant to generate rental income, the design should prioritize durability, efficiency, and broad market appeal.

Key design priorities usually include:

- A simple, efficient layout
- Durable, low maintenance materials
- Standard fixtures taht are easy to repair or replace

The goal is not luxury—it is long-term reliability and consistent demand.

Renters value comfort and functionality far more than custom finishes. A clean, well-designed space with durable materials will outperform a flashy but fragile design over time.

Option 2: Family Use

When the ADU is designed for a family member, you gain more flexibility—and more responsibility—to design for specific needs.

Common priorities include:

- Fewer stairs or step-free accessAesthetics or architectural style
- Wider doors or walk-in showers
- Extra storage
- A closer visual or physical connection to the main house

Here, comfort and daily usability matter more than resale value or rental trends:
Even if your family member is mobile today, thoughtful accessibility features can prevent costly retrofits later..

Option 3: Home Office or Studio

If your ADU will function as a workspace, the design should support focus, comfort, and productivity.

Important features may include

- Ample natural light
- Sound insulation
- Reliable, high-speed internet
- Flexible interior layout

In many cases, a full kitchen is not required—reducing both square footage and construction costs.

> *Bigger is not always better—especially when it comes to ADUs.*

While California law allows homeowners to build ADUs of at least 800 square feet even on smaller lots, the most cost-effective projects often stay smaller.

The 500-750 Square Foot “Sweet Spot”

Many experienced builders and designers agree that this range offers the best balance:

- Large enough for a comfortable one-bedroom or compact two-bedroom layout
- Small enough to keep construction, labor, and material costs under control

Using Space Efficiently

Smart design matters more than total square footage. Work with your designer to:

- Minimize or eliminate long hallways
- Favor open kitchen and living areasUse vertical storage such as tall cabinets or shelving

Every Square Foot Should Earn Its Keep

> *If a space does not serve a clear purpose, it is quietly increasing your cost without adding value.*

Exterior Style: Bleeding In or Standing Out

Your ADU’s exterior appearance affects cost, approvals, and construction complexity.

Matching the Main House

Some homeowners prefer their ADU to look like a natural extension of the existing home. This may involve:

- Matching rooflines
- Using similar siding materials
- Choosing comparable windows and finishes

While visually cohesive, this approach can increase design and construction complexity

Simple Modern Design

A clean, modern exterior is often the most affordable option to build.

Simple forms and rooflines:

- Reduce construction complexity
- Lower framing and roofing costs
- Speed up the build process

Simplicity Saves Money

Fewer angles, fewer materials, and fewer decorative details usually mean fewer surprises—and fewer budget overruns

Why You Need a CLear "Design Brief"

Professionals work best when expectations are written, not assumed.

Before meeting with any architect or engineer, create a Design Brief—a short written document that explains what you want and what matters most. This single step can prevent weeks of redesign and thousands of dollars in revisions.

Your Design Brief should include:

- Incomplete submissions are so dangerous
- Vague “missing items” comments are often used to delay

Project Goals

What is the primary purpose of the ADU?

Examples:

- “Generate long-term rental income”
- “Create a comfortable home for my parents”

Target Bugdet

A realistic total construction budget (excluding land value and professional fees).

Must-Have Features

Non-negotiable items, such as:

- Two bedrooms
- Full bathroom
- Washer/dryer hookups

Nice-to-Have Features

Items that can be removed if needed:

- Deck or patio

- Skylights
- Custom finishes

Sahring this document with your design team keeps everyone aligned and dramatically reduces costly misunderstandings.

Scripts & Questions You Can Use

Your First Design Meeting

"Our primary goal for this ADU is __________. Our total construction budget is __________. These features are non-negotiable, and these are optional if we need to reduce costs."

Key Questions to Ask Yourself

- Who will live here five years from now?
- Is this ADU meant to generate income or serve family first?
- What features would be hardest or most expensive to change later?

Key Questions to Ask Professionals

- "Which parts of this design add the most cost?"
- "Where can we simplify without hurting function?"
- "What assumptions are you making that we should confirm now?"

Defining Your ADU Vision: Chapter Checklist

Before moving to the next chapter, confirm that you have:

- ☐ Defined the primary purpose of your ADU
- ☐ Identified your ideal size range
- ☐ Decided on a general exterior style
- ☐ Listed must-have and nice-to-have features
- ☐ Written a one-page Design Brief

Take Action this Week

1. Write your one-page Design Brief (even if it feels rough).
2. Rank your top three priorities for the ADU.
3. Identify one feature you are willing to remove if costs increase.

FINAL TAKEAWAY

A clear vision is not a limitation—it is your strongest tool for staying on budget, avoiding stress, and building an ADU that truly works.

CHAPTER 2

HIRING YOUR DESIGN & ENGINEERING TEAM

In reviewing hundreds of ADU projects across Southern California, one truth becomes unavoidable: the quality of your plans determines the success of your build far more than the tools you use or the contractor you hire.

In the **Design-Driven DIY approach**, your design and engineering team is the **single most important investment** you will make. These professionals create the documents that allow you—the homeowner—to manage construction with confidence.

When plans are clear, detailed, and accurate:

- Builders work faster
- Fewer questions arise in the field
- Costly mistakes and rework are avoided

When plans are vague or incomplete, even a small ADU can become stressful, slow, and expensive.

This is **not** the place to look for the cheapest option. The real goal is to hire professionals who understand ADUs deeply and can deliver plans that are:

- Easy for builders and trades to follow

- Fully compliant with local and state codes
- Likely to pass city plan review with minimal revisions.

Think of Your Design Team as Your Project Manager on Paper

Every decision you don't have to make during construction saves time, money, and stress. Good plans do that work in advance.

Architect, Designer, or Drafter: Who Do You Actually Need?

One of the most common homeowner mistakes is hiring the wrong type of design professional for the project.

The word "designer" is used loosely, but not all design professionals offer the same services or expertise. Understanding the difference helps you avoid overpaying—or under-hiring.

Architect

An architect is a **licensed professional** trained to manage complex designs and regulatory challenges. Architects are usually needed when:

- The lot has unusual zoning or site constraints
- The design is highly customized or architecturally complex
- The project requires variances or special approvals

Architects often provide full-service design and coordination, but they are typically the **most expensive option**.

If your ADU is straightforward, hiring an architect may add cost without adding proportional value.

Building Designer or Draftsperson

For most ADUs, a skilled building designer or draftsperson is the best fit.

An experienced ADU designer can:

- Produce high-quality, code-compliant plans
- Work efficiently within standard ADU regulations
- Cost significantly less than a full architectural service

For typical ADU projects, this option offers the **best balance of cost, speed, and expertise**.

Pre-Approved Plan Providers

Some cities in Southern California offer **pre-approved ADU plans**. These plans have already passed city review, which can mean:

- Faster permit approval
- Lower design costs

The tradeoff is limited flexibility. You can often make minor adjustments, but the layout and exterior style are mostly fixed.

Speed vs. Customization

pre-approved plans are ideal if your lot fits standard conditions and you are comfortable with fewer design choices

Why ADU Experience Matters So Much

Southern California is one of the most regulated building environments in the country.

Your plans must comply with:

- Local zoning ordinances
- Seismic (earthquake) standards
- Title 24 energy efficiency requirements

A firm that **specializes in ADUs in your specific county**—such as Los Angeles, Orange County, or San Diego—brings a major advantage. These teams already know:

- What local plan reviewers typically flag
- How to avoid common permit delays
- The most cost-effective ways to meet code

Local Knowledge Saves Time

Experience with your city's planning department can shave weeks—or months—off the approval process

Contracts: What Must Be Clearly Defined

Misunderstandings almost always come from vague contracts.

Before signing anything, make sure the agreement clearly explains what you are paying for and exactly what you will receive.

Fixed Fee vs. Hourly Billing

For homeowners, a fixed-fee contract is usually the safest option. It provides cost certainty and avoids surprise invoices.

Confirm that the fee includes:

- Revisions required by the city

- Updates needed to pass plan check

If revisions are billed separately, get that clearly defined in writing.

Required Deliverables

Your contract should list all final documents, including:

- Architectural drawings (floor plans, elevations, sections)
- Structural engineering drawings and calculations
- Title 24 energy compliance documents
- A site plan showing utilities and property layout
- A complete plan set ready for city submission

Never assume a document is part of the package unless it appears in the contract.

Verifying Licenses and Checking References

Professional credentials protect you—and your project.

Always verify licenses through:

- The California Architects Board
- The California Board for Professional Engineers

Next, request references from at least three recent ADU projects. When speaking with past clients, ask practical questions:

Questions to Ask References

- "How many revisions were required before approval?"
- "Did the plans pass city review on the first try?"
- "Were the plans clear for the builder to follow?"
- "Would you hire this team again?"

Clear, confident answers are a strong sign you are hiring the right team

Scripts You Can Use Immediately

Script for Initial Design Calls

"This is an ADU project in __________ County. We plan to manage construction ourselves, so we need clear, builder-friendly plans that pass plan check efficiently."

Script for Contract Clarification

"Can you walk me through exactly what deliverables are included and how city-required revisions are handled?"

Key Questions for Your Design Team

- "Where do ADU projects like this usually get delayed?"
- "What design choices reduce construction cost?"
- "What assumptions should we confirm now?"

Hiring the Right Team: Chapter Checklist

Before moving forward, confirm that you have:

- ☐ Chosen the right type of design professional
- ☐ Verified all licenses
- ☐ Reviewed recent ADU references
- ☐ Confirmed a fixed-fee contract
- ☐ Listed all required deliverables in writing

Take Action This Week

1. Identify whether your ADU truly requires an architect—or not.
2. Call at least two ADU-focused designers in your county.
3. Request a sample plan set to evaluate clarity and details

Final Takeaway

Great plans don't just meet code—they guide your entire project. When your plans are right, managing your own ADU becomes achievable, predictable, and far less stressful.

CHAPTER 3

STRUCTURAL ENGINEERING: THE BLUEPRINT FOR DIY SUCCESS

Across successful owner-built ADU projects, one factor consistently separates smooth builds from stressful ones: clear, well-engineered structural plans that are followed exactly.

In the Design-Driven DIY approach, the structural engineer is one of your most important partners. Their work establishes the non-negotiable rules of your project. These plans define how your ADU must be built so it is safe, legal, and strong enough to withstand Southern California's earthquakes and soil conditions.

Think of the structural plans as the instruction manual that keeps your building standing. On the job site, these drawings outrank opinions, shortcuts, and "this is how we usually do it." As an owner-builder, learning how to read the basics of these plans allows you to manage contractors with confidence and avoid costly—and dangerous—mistakes.

Structural plans are not design preferences. They are engineered requirements backed by law and physics

Because California is one of the most earthquake-prone regions in the country, every ADU must be designed and stamped by a licensed structural engineer.

Your structural engineer is responsible for:

- Designing the foundation system
- Determining how walls, floors, and roofs are framed
- Creating systems that resist earthquake forces, known as shear walls

Trying to build without a licensed engineer's stamp is not just risky—it is illegal. The city will reject your plans immediately, and construction will not be allowed to proceed.

More importantly, skipping this step puts both human safety and your financial investment at serious risk.

> *If the plans are not stamped by a licensed engineer, the project stops before it starts.*

How to Read Structural Plans (Without Being an Engineer)

You do not need to understand the math—you need to understand the instructions.

Structural drawings can look intimidating, but they are simply a set of detailed directions. As an owner-builder, your goal is not to redesign the structure—it is to ensure it is built exactly as drawn.

Focus on these key areas.

Foundation Details

The foundation drawings tell your concrete contractor exactly how the building connects to the ground, including:

- The depth and width of footings
- The size, spacing, and placement of steel reinforcement (rebar)
- The location of anchor bolts that tie the framing to the concrete

These details are critical. If they are ignored or altered, the entire structure above is compromised.

Mistakes Below Grade Are the Most Expensive. Foundation errors are difficult—and sometimes impossible—to fix once concrete is poured.

Shear Wall Details

Shear walls are specially reinforced walls that prevent the building from moving sideways during an earthquake.

The plans will specify:

- The exact location of each shear wall
- The type and thickness of wood sheathing
- The precise nailing pattern
- Required metal connectors and hold-downs

These instructions must be followed exactly. Substituting fasteners or changing layouts without approval is a common—and serious—error.

Load-Bearing Areas

Structural plans also show how weight travels from the roof and floors down to the foundation.

This includes:

- Beam and header sizes above doors and windows
- Which walls are structural and cannot be moved or altered

Understanding this protects you from well-intended but dangerous field changes.

Not All Walls Are Equal. Removing or modifying a load-bearing wall without engineering approval can compromise the entire building.

How a Good Engineer Makes DIY Easier

Good engineering is not about adding material—it is about adding clarity.

An experienced structural engineer who understands ADUs and the Design-Driven DIY approach designs structures that are both strong and practical.

A good engineer will:

- Use standard materials readily available at local suppliers
- Avoid unnecessary complexity that slows construction
- Balance safety and cost, preventing over-engineering

When done well, the structural plans:

- Reduce confusion on site
- Speed up inspections

- Give you confidence when managing trades

Simple Structures Build Faster. Clear, efficient engineering saves time, labor, and money—without sacrificing safety.

Scripts You Can Use Immediately

Script for Your Structural Engineer

"We plan to manage construction ourselves, so we need structural plans that are clear, buildable, and easy for trades to follow."

Script for Contractors

"We are building strictly per the structural plans. If something needs to change, we'll confirm it with the engineer first."

Key Questions to Ask

- "Which details are most commonly built incorrectly?"
- "Where should we be extra careful during framing?"
- "What site inspections should we never skip?"

Structural Readiness: Chapter Checklist

Before construction begins, confirm that you have:

- ☐ Structural plans stamped by a licensed engineer
- ☐ Reviewed foundation, shear wall, and load-bearing details
- ☐ Shared structural plans with all relevant trades

- ☐ Understood which elements cannot be changed on site

Take Action This Week

1. Review your structural plans page by page—even if you don't understand every note.
2. Highlight shear walls, foundations, and load-bearing elements.
3. Ask your engineer one clarifying question now, not during construction.

FINAL TAKEAWAY

Structural plans are the backbone of your ADU. When you respect them, understand them, and enforce them on site, DIY construction becomes far safer, smoother, and more predictable

CHAPTER 4

TITLE 24: CALIFORNIA'S ENERGY CODE

In permit reviews across California, Title 24 is one of the most common reasons projects are delayed—not because it is complicated, but because it is misunderstood or ignored.

Title 24 is California's statewide energy efficiency code, and it applies to every new ADU. It is not optional. Its purpose is to reduce energy use by setting minimum standards for how buildings are insulated, heated, cooled, and powered.

In practical terms, Title 24 determines many of the exact products you will use in your ADU—insulation, windows, lighting, and mechanical systems. As an owner-builder, understanding the basics of Title 24 helps you make smart purchasing decisions and avoid failed inspections later.

Title 24 Controls What You Buy. Even small substitutions can cause an inspection failure if they don't match the report.

What a Title 24 Report Is (and Why It Matters)

Think of the Title 24 report as the energy rulebook for your project. Your design team will provide a **Title 24 energy compliance report.** This technical document proves your ADU meets California's energy requirements and is reviewed by the city during plan check and inspections.

The report does not make recommendations. It sets **minimum performance requirements** that must be followed exactly.

Inspectors will reference this report to verify that what was installed matches what was approved.

The Inspector Has the Same Report You Do. If the product installed doesn't match the report, the inspection fails—no matter how well everything else is built.

Key Items Covered in a Title 24 Report

You don't need to understand every calculation, but you must understand what the report controls. These are the most common elements.

Insulation

The report lists required insulation levels for:

- Walls
- Ceilings (and sometimes floors)

These levels are shown as **R-values**, which measure resistance to heat flow. Higher R-values mean better insulation and lower energy loss.

Windows

Windows must meet specific energy performance standards. The report will specify:

- **U-factor** – how much heat passes through the window
- **Solar Heat Gain Coefficient (SHGC)** – how much heat from sunlight enters the space

In most cases, this requires high-performance, dual-pane windows.

"Looks Similar" Is Not the Same as "Compliant". Two windows can look identical and still fail Title 24 if their ratings differ.

Heating and Cooling (HVAC)

Title 24 regulates the efficiency of heating and cooling systems. The report specifies acceptable efficiency ratings, so the system uses less energy while maintaining comfort.

Installing a cheaper or older system—even if it fits—can result in a failed inspection.

Water Heater

Water heaters must meet efficiency requirements. Many ADUs use tankless water heaters because they:

- Meet efficiency standards
- Save space

Other compliant options may be allowed, but they must match the report exactly.

Lighting

Title 24 requires high-efficiency lighting, typically LED fixtures. This applies to:

- Most interior lighting
- Some exterior fixtures

Using non-compliant fixtures is a common and avoidable mistake.

How Title 24 Affects You as a DIY Builder

Title 24 is one of the most common places owner-builders get tripped up.

As the homeowner, you are responsible for ensuring that installed materials **match the Title 24 report exactly.**

If you install:

- Windows with lower efficiency ratings
- A water heater that does not meet specifications
- Lighting that is not Title 24 compliant

Your project will fail inspection—even if everything else is perfect.

Inspectors compare what is installed in the ADU to what appears in the report.

Treat Title 24 Like a Checklist, not a Suggestion. Deviating from the report leads to rework, delays, and extra cost.

The Simplest Way to Succeed with Title 24

The safest and smartest approach is straightforward:

- Use the Title 24 report as a shopping list
- Use it again as an installation checklist
- Do not substitute products without written confirmation from your design team

When followed precisely, Title 24 inspections are usually fast and uneventful.

Scripts & Questions You Can Use

Script for Suppliers

"This product must match the Title 24 energy report exactly. Can you confirm the U-factor, SHGC, or efficiency rating in writing?"

Script for Contractors

"We are installing exactly what's listed in the Title 24 report. Any changes must be approved before installation."

Questions to Ask Your Design Team

- "Which items are most commonly installed incorrectly?"
- "What substitutions require an updated report?"
- "Can you flag any items that are easy to miss during purchasing?"

Title 24 Readiness: Chapter Checklist

Before inspections, confirm that you have:

- ☐ A final Title 24 report approved by the city
- ☐ Verified insulation R-values
- ☐ Confirmed window ratings match the report
- ☐ Installed compliant HVAC and water-heating systems
- ☐ Used Title 24-approved lighting fixtures

Take Action This Week

1. Read your Title 24 report and highlight every item that affects purchasing.
2. Confirm product specifications before buying—never after.
3. Ask one clarifying question now to avoid a failed inspection later.

FINAL TAKEAWAY

Title 24 is not about preference—it is about compliance. When you treat the report as a contract, your inspections become predictable and stress-fre

PART II

NAVIGATING THE BUREAUCRACY (PERMIT-TING & SITE PREP

CHAPTER 5

PERMIT EXPEDITION: GETTING APPROVED FASTER

In ADU projects across California, permits are rarely denied—but they are often delayed. The difference between a smooth approval and a stalled one is usually preparation, not luck.

Once your design, structural, and energy plans are complete, the next step is obtaining a **building permit**. This permit is the city's official authorization to begin construction.

While California has streamlined ADU approvals in recent years, local building departments still operate on their own timelines and procedures. For first-time owner-builders, the process can feel slow, confusing, and opaque.

This chapter explains what the permit process actually looks like, which delays are normal, and how to move through approvals as efficiently as possible.

Permits Are a Process, not a Moment. Expect reviews, comments, and revisions. This is standard—not a sign of failure.

The Permit Process: Step by Step

Although every city has its quirks, ADU permits almost always follow the same basic path.

Understanding the sequence removes uncertainty and helps you respond quickly.

Step 1: Plan Submission

You submit a complete plan set to your local planning or building department. This usually includes:

- Architectural drawings
- Structural engineering plans
- Title 24 energy compliance report

Incomplete submissions are one of the most common causes of delays.

Incomplete Plans Equal Automatic Delays. Missing documents often send your application to the back of the line.

Step 2: Plan Review (Plan Check)

A city reviewer—often called a **plan checker**—examines your plans to verify compliance with state and local building codes.

This review is detailed and methodical. Even for a small ADU, it is normal for this stage to take time.

Step 3: Comments and Corrections

In most cases, the city will return your plans with a list of required changes or clarifications.

This is **normal**.

These comments may address:

- Code interpretations
- Missing notes or details
- Clarifications on structural or energy items

Your design team revises the plans, responds to each comment, and resubmits them for review.

Comments Are Not Criticism

> *Plan check comments are part of the system—not a judgment on your project.*

Step 4: Permit Approval

Once all comments are addressed and accepted, the city issues your building permit.

At this point, you are legally allowed to begin construction.

No Permit Means No Work. Starting construction early can lead to stop-work orders, fines, and serious delays.

How a Permit Expediter Can Help

A permit expediter speaks the language of city departments, so you don't have to.

A **permit expediter** is a professional who manages the permit process on your behalf. For a fee, they typically handle:

- Submitting plans
- Tracking review status
- Following up with city departments
- Coordinating responses and resubmissions

Permit expediters understand how local departments operate, what reviewers commonly flag, and how to avoid preventable slowdowns. Many have established working relationships with city staff, which helps keep applications moving.

Is a Permit Expediter Worth It for DIY Builders?

For many Design-Driven DIY builders, the answer is yes—especially if:

- You are working full-time
- Your city has a backlog
- You want to focus on construction preparation instead of paperwork

Hiring an expediter allows you to:

- Order materials earlier
- Line up subcontractors
- Build a realistic construction schedule

Time Is a Hidden Cost. Weeks spent waiting for approvals can delay rentals, increase material prices, and stall momentum.

Used strategically, permit expedition can save **weeks—or even months—of downtime**.

Scripts You Can Use Immediately

Script for the Building Department

"I'm calling to confirm the current status of our ADU plan review and whether any additional information is needed."

Script for a Permit Expediter

"This is a Design-Driven DIY ADU. We have a complete plan set and want to move through plan check efficiently."

Questions to Ask

- "What is the current average review time?"
- "Are corrections reviewed in order of resubmittal?"
- "Are digital or over-the-counter approvals available?"

Permit Readiness: Chapter Checklist

Before submitting, confirm that you have:

- ☐ A complete, coordinated plan set
- ☐ Structural and Title 24 documents included
- ☐ Clear contact information for your design team
- ☐ A plan for handling city comments quickly

Take Action This Week

1. Confirm submission requirements with your local building department.
2. Ask your design team about typical review timelines.
3. Decide whether a permit expediter makes financial sense for your schedule.

FINAL TAKEAWAY

Permits don't stall projects—lack of preparation does. When you understand the process and manage it actively, approvals become predictable instead of frustrating.

CHAPTER 6

THE OWNER-BUILDER PERMIT: UNDERSTANDING YOUR LEGAL ROLE

Thousands of homeowners successfully build ADUs as owner-builders every year—but the ones who succeed understand their legal role before construction begins, not after.

When you choose to build your ADU as an owner-builder, you are formally stepping into the role that a general contractor would normally fill. This decision can save a significant amount of money, but it also comes with legal responsibilities that cannot be ignored.

This chapter explains what the owner-builder role actually means, what you are legally responsible for, and how to protect yourself throughout the build.

Owner-Builder Is a Legal Status, not a Title. The city does not see you as "helping out." It sees you as the person in charge.

What Does "Owner-Builder" Mean?

An **owner-builder** is a property owner who acts as their own general contractor. Instead of hiring one company to manage the entire project, you take on that role yourself.

As an owner-builder, you are responsible for:

- Coordinating the overall project
- Hiring and scheduling subcontractors (concrete, framing, plumbing, electrical, etc.)
- Ordering materials
- Ensuring all work follows approved plans and building codes

You do not need to perform the physical labor yourself—but you are legally responsible for how the project is managed.

Management Is the Job. Even if you never pick up a tool, you are still the contractor in the eyes of the city.

Your Key Legal Responsibilities

When you sign as an owner-builder, responsibility does not disappear—it concentrates.

The city and state will look to you if something goes wrong. Understanding these obligations upfront allows you to manage risk instead of reacting to it.

Job Site Safety

You are responsible for maintaining a reasonably safe construction site. This includes:

- Ensuring workers follow basic safety practices
- Addressing obvious hazards on the property
- Coordinating work so unsafe conditions are not created

While licensed subcontractors must follow their own safety regulations, ultimate responsibility for site conditions rests with you.

Safety Is Shared, Responsibility Is Not. Subcontractors must work safely—but the owner-builder is accountable for the site.

Insurance Coverage

Insurance is one of the most important protections you have as an owner-builder.

You should:

- Maintain homeowner's insurance that includes construction-related liability
- Verify that every subcontractor carries:
    - General liability insurance
    - Workers' compensation insurance

> *Never assume coverage. Always request proof of insurance before work begins.*

No Proof, No Work. If a subcontractor cannot provide insurance certificates, do not allow them on site.

Building Code Compliance

Even though licensed professionals perform the work, you are responsible for ensuring the ADU is built according to:

- Approved plans
- State and local building codes

- Required inspections

If something fails inspection, it is your responsibility to coordinate corrections and schedule re-inspection.

Inspections Protect You. Failed inspections are not punishment—they are safeguards.

Protecting Yourself as an Owner-Builder

Being an owner-builder does not mean taking unnecessary risks—it means managing them intentionally.

The safest approach includes:

- Hiring licensed and insured subcontractors only
- Following approved plans exactly
- Scheduling and passing all required inspections
- Keeping written records of:
    - Contracts
    - Insurance certificates
    - Payments and receipts

These habits protect you legally and financially.

Scripts & Questions You Can Use

Script for Subcontractors

"Before we schedule work, I'll need copies of your license, liability insurance, and workers' comp."

Script for Inspectors

"We are building strictly per the approved plans and are ready for inspection."

Questions to Ask Yourself

- "Do I have documentation for everyone working on site?"
- "Have I scheduled all required inspections?"
- "Is this change approved—or just convenient?"

Owner-Builder Readiness: Chapter Checklist

Before construction begins, confirm that you have:

- ☐ Signed the owner-builder permit knowingly
- ☐ Confirmed insurance coverage
- ☐ Verified licenses and insurance for all subcontractors
- ☐ A system for scheduling inspections
- ☐ Organized project records

Take Action This Week

1. Review your homeowner's insurance policy and confirm construction coverage.
2. Create a simple folder (digital or physical) for licenses and insurance certificates.
3. List all inspections required for your ADU.

FINAL TAKEAWAY

The owner-builder role gives you control and savings—but only when you understand and manage your legal responsibilities. Knowledge is what turns risk into confidence.

CHAPTER 7

SITE PREPARATION: MANAGING YOUR FIRST SUBCONTRACTORS

In successful owner-built ADU projects, the earliest construction work often determines how smoothly everything that follows will go.

Once your permit is approved, construction can officially begin. This phase—**site preparation**—is when work starts on the ground itself. It is also your first real test as an owner-builder, because you will be hiring, scheduling, and coordinating multiple subcontractors for the first time.

This chapter explains who you need to hire, what each subcontractor does, and how to manage this phase confidently and efficiently.

Early Mistakes Compound

Errors made during site preparation are difficult and expensive to fix later.

Who You'll Hire for Site Preparation

Site preparation is a sequence, not a single task.

Several specialized subcontractors are typically involved, and their work must occur in the correct order.

Demolition and Grading

If existing structures, concrete, or landscaping are in the way, a **demolition crew** removes them. A **grading contractor** then prepares the site by leveling the ground according to the approved plans.

This step ensures proper drainage and sets accurate elevations for the foundation.

Trenching and Utilities

Trenching creates pathways for:

- Water
- Sewer
- Gas
- Electrical lines

These trenches must follow approved plans and are often inspected before being backfilled.

Never Cover a Trench Without Inspection. Backfilling too early almost always results in rework and delays.

Concrete and Foundation Work

The **concrete contractor** builds the foundation that supports the entire ADU. This includes:

- Footings
- Slabs
- Steel reinforcement (rebar)
- Anchor bolts specified in the structural plans

This is one of the most critical phases of the entire project.

Concrete Locks in Mistakes. Once concrete is poured, changes are expensive—or impossible.

You may hire:

- One company to handle multiple tasks, or
- Separate subcontractors for each scope

Either approach can work as long as responsibilities are clearly defined in writing.

How to Hire the Right Subcontractors

Even without a general contractor, professional standards still apply.

Before hiring anyone:

- Verify their license with the state
- Confirm liability and workers' compensation insurance
- Ask for references from recent, similar projects
- Use a written contract that clearly defines scope, schedule, and payment terms

Never rely on verbal agreements.

Clear Contracts Prevent Conflict. If expectations aren't written down, they will be interpreted differently on site.

Managing the Site Preparation Phase

Your job as owner-builder is coordination, not constant supervision.

Good organization and communication make this phase manageable.

Clear Communication

Provide each subcontractor with:

- Relevant plan pages
- A clear description of their scope of work
- Any inspection requirements related to their task

Do not assume they will "figure it out."

Clarity Is a Form of Leadership. Clear instructions reduce mistakes and protect your schedule.

Scheduling and Coordination

Site preparation follows a strict sequence:

- Grading must be complete before trenching
- Trenching must pass inspection before concrete work
- Foundation inspections must occur before pouring

You are responsible for ensuring tasks happen in the correct order.

Checking Quality and Progress

Visit the site regularly—especially before:

- Trenches are backfilled
- Concrete is poured

Look for:

- Work that matches approved plans
- Clean and organized job conditions
- Issues that need immediate attention

> *Catching problems early is far easier than fixing them later.*

Inspect Before It Disappears. Anything covered up is harder to verify and fix.

Why Site Preparation Matters So Much

Everything above ground depends on what happens below it.

When site preparation is done correctly:

- Inspections go smoother
- Framing starts on time
- Fewer surprises appear later

With clear communication, careful scheduling, and basic oversight, even a first-time owner-builder can manage this phase successfully.

Scripts You Can Use Immediately

Script for Subcontractors

"We are building strictly per the approved plans. Please review these sheets before starting."

Script for Inspectors

"Trenching/foundation work is complete and ready for inspection."

Questions to Ask

- "What needs to be inspected before this is covered?"
- "Does this match the plan exactly?"
- "Is anything unclear before we move forward?"

Chapter 7 Checklist: Site Preparation Readiness

Before moving to framing, confirm that you have:

- ☐ Completed demolition and grading per plans
- ☐ Passed all required trench inspections
- ☐ Installed foundation elements per structural drawings
- ☐ Documented work before it was covered
- ☐ Coordinated the next phase of construction

Take Action This Week

1. Create a simple site-prep schedule with inspection points.
2. Confirm subcontractor scopes in writing.
3. Walk the site before every inspection or pour.

FINAL TAKEAWAY

Site preparation sets the physical and organizational foundation for your ADU. When you manage this phase carefully, the rest of the build becomes faster, cleaner, and far less stressful.

PART III

THE OWNER-BUILDER'S CONSTRUCTION ROADMAP

CHAPTER 8

FOUNDATION & SLAB: MANAGING THE CONCRETE CREW

In ADU projects that run into major structural or budget problems, the foundation is often where the first mistake was made—and locked in permanently.

The foundation and slab phase are one of the **most critical stages** of your entire ADU project. Once concrete is poured, errors are difficult, expensive, and sometimes impossible to correct. That is why careful preparation and focused oversight during this phase are essential.

As an owner-builder, you do not need to be a concrete expert. You do need to understand **what must be in place, when inspections are required, and how to confirm the work matches your approved plans.**

This chapter walks through the foundation process in three clear stages:

- Before the pour
- During the pour
- After the pour

Concrete Is Permanent. This is not the phase to "hope it's right." Verification happens before the truck arrives.

Before the Pour: Your Pre-Pour Checklist

Most concrete problems begin before any concrete is placed.

Before the pour, several critical items must be completed, reviewed, and approved.

Forms Are Set Correctly

Concrete forms shape the foundation and slab. Confirm that:

- The layout matches the approved plans
- Footing depths and widths match the structural drawings
- Slab thickness matches the engineer's specifications

Forms Control Everything. If the forms are wrong, the concrete will be wrong—no matter how good the crew is.

Rebar and Steel Reinforcement Are Installed

Steel reinforcement gives concrete its strength. Check that:

- Rebar size and spacing match the structural plans
- Rebar is properly tied
- Rebar is supported on chairs or spacers (not resting on soil)

Improper rebar placement is a common inspection failure.

Anchor Bolts and Hold-Downs Are in Place

These components connect the framing to the foundation and resist earthquake forces.

Verify that:

- Anchor bolts and hold-downs are installed in the correct locations
- Spacing matches the engineer's drawings
- Required hardware is on site before the pour

Missing Hardware = Costly Rework. Drilling anchors later is slower, weaker, and often rejected by inspectors.

Underground Utilities Are Complete

Before concrete is poured, all under-slab work must be finished, including:

- Plumbing lines
- Electrical conduits
- Grounding components

Nothing should be added under the slab after the pour.

Required Inspections Are Passed

Most cities require a pre-pour inspection.

Do not allow concrete placement until:

- The inspector has reviewed the work
- Approval is given to proceed

No Inspection, No Pour. Pouring early almost always results in removal and replacement.

During the Pour: What to Watch For

Concrete day moves fast, but your presence matters.

You are not directing the crew—you are confirming that the plan is being followed.

Proper Placement

Concrete should be placed:

- Evenly
- Continuously
- Without gaps or segregation

Watch for rushed placement or skipped areas.

Correct Slab Height and Level

Confirm:

- Even distribution
- Smooth, level surfaces
- No obvious low or high spots

These issues affect framing, doors, and finishes later.

Vibration and Consolidation

The crew should use vibration tools to:

- Remove air pockets
- Fully surround rebar and anchor bolts

This is especially important at edges and connections.

Weather Awareness

Weather affects curing and strength.

Ask how the crew plans to:

- Protect concrete from extreme heat
- Cover it during rain
- Prevent rapid drying

Weather Changes the Rules. Good crews plan for conditions—bad ones react too late.

After the Pour: Post-Pour Quality Checks

The pour is not the finish line. Once the concrete is placed, confirm the following before moving forward.

Curing Process

Concrete gains strength over time.

Confirm that:

- The slab is kept moist if required
- Curing time follows the engineer's recommendations
- No framing begins too early

Anchor Bolt Alignment

Check that anchor bolts are:

- Straight
- At the correct height
- Properly exposed—not buried or leaning

Misaligned bolts create delays during framing.

Surface Condition

Inspect for:

- Excessive cracking
- Uneven areas
- Edges that do not match the forms

Hairline cracks are normal. Larger cracks or settlement issues should be addressed immediately.

Early Fixes Are Easier. Waiting only makes concrete issues harder to resolve.

Why This Phase Is So Important

Everything above the slab depends on what happens here.

A properly built foundation:

- Supports the structure safely
- Makes framing faster and cleaner
- Reduces inspection issues later

Taking the time to verify each step protects the entire project. When the foundation is done right, the rest of the ADU has a far better chance of staying on schedule and on budget.

Scripts You Can Use Immediately

Script for the Concrete Crew

"We're building strictly per the approved plans. Please confirm everything is ready before the inspector and the pour."

Script for the Inspector

"All pre-pour items are complete and ready for inspection."

Questions to Ask

- "Is anything missing before we pour?"
- "Does this match the structural drawings exactly?"
- "What curing steps will you follow?"

Chapter 8 Checklist: Foundation Readiness

Before framing begins, confirm that you have:

☐ Passed all required pre-pour inspections

☐ Verified rebar, anchor bolts, and forms

☐ Confirmed proper concrete placement and curing

☐ Documented the foundation with photos

☐ Addressed any issues immediately

Take Action This Week

1. Review your structural foundation drawings in detail.
2. Walk the site the day before the pour.
3. Plan to be present—or represented—on pour day.

FINAL TAKEAWAY

The foundation is not just concrete—it is the physical commitment to your plans. When you manage this phase carefully, everything that follows becomes easier to build and easier to inspect.

CHAPTER 9

FRAMING: SUPERVISING THE SKELETON

In well-run ADU projects, framing is the moment when good planning finally becomes visible—and when mistakes can either be fixed easily or locked in quickly.

Framing is the stage where your ADU starts to look like a building. Walls go up, the roof takes shape, and room sizes and ceiling heights become real. This phase moves fast and sets the structure for everything that follows—plumbing, electrical, insulation, drywall, and finishes.

As an owner-builder, your role is **not** to swing a hammer. Your role is to ensure framing is done **safely, accurately, and exactly according to the approved plans**. This chapter explains how to hire a framing crew, understand what they are building, and know what should be happening each day.

Framing Sets the Rules for Every Trade. If framing is off, every trade that follows pays the price.

Hiring a Framing Crew

Framing errors are structural errors.

Framing crews build the structural "skeleton" of the ADU using wood or steel. Because this work directly affects safety, inspections, and future trades, choosing the right crew is critical.

When hiring a framing crew:

- Verify their contractor's license and insurance
- Ask for references from recent framing projects
- Confirm experience with ADUs or small residential buildings
- Use a written agreement that defines:
    - Scope of work
    - Schedule
    - Payment terms

Avoid crews that promise to "build it their way."

Plans Over Preference. Framing must follow the structural engineer's drawings—not habit or convenience.

Understanding the Framing Plans (What You Need to Know)

You don't need to frame the building—you need to recognize when it's framed incorrectly.

Focus on these core elements.

Wall Layouts

The plans show:

- Wall locations
- Which walls are structural (load bearing)

- Wall thicknesses and stud spacing

Structural walls cannot be moved or altered without engineering approval.

Not All Walls Are Moveable. Changing a structural wall without approval is a serious violation.

Beams and Headers

Headers are beams above doors and windows.

The plans specify:

- Size
- Material
- Location

Improper headers are a common cause of failed inspections.

Shear Walls and Hardware

Shear walls resist earthquake forces.

The plans detail:

- Which walls are shear walls
- Nailing patterns
- Required metal connectors and hold-downs

These details must be followed exactly.

Shear Details Are Non-Negotiable. Substituting nails or skipping hardware can stop the project.

Roof Framing

The plans show:

- Roof type and slope
- Rafter or truss sizes
- Required connections between roof and walls

Roof framing errors affect both structure and waterproofing.

A Simple Day-by-Day Framing Overview

While every project varies, framing usually follows a predictable rhythm.

Day 1: Layout and Bottom Plates

- Wall locations are marked on the slab
- Bottom plates are anchored to the foundation

Day 2–3: Wall Framing

- Walls are built flat and raised into position
- Door and window openings are framed

Day 4: Shear Walls and Hardware

- Shear wall panels are installed
- Metal connectors and hold-downs are placed per plans

Day 5: Roof Framing

- Rafters or trusses are installed
- Roof shape becomes visible

Day 6: Sheathing

- Exterior walls and roof are sheathed
- The structure stiffens and prepares for inspection

Inspections Happen at Milestones. Don't let the crew move ahead before inspections are complete.

Your Role During Framing

Your job is verification, coordination, and timing.

As the owner-builder, you should:

- Confirm framing matches approved plans
- Verify required hardware is installed
- Schedule framing inspections at the correct time
- Address questions or discrepancies immediately

Walk the site daily if possible. Small framing errors are easy to fix early—but expensive later.

Inspect Before It's Covered. Once insulation and drywall go in, framing errors are hidden and harder to fix.

Why Framing Matters So Much

Framing determines far more than just structure.

It affects:

- Structural safety
- Room dimensions and ceiling heights
- Ease of plumbing, electrical, and insulation installation

When framing is accurate, every phase that follows becomes simpler and faster. When it's rushed or altered, problems multiply quickly.

Scripts & Questions You Can Use

Script for the Framing Crew

"We're building strictly per the structural plans. Let me know before making any changes."

Script for Inspectors

"Framing and shear hardware are complete and ready for inspection."

Questions to Ask

- "Does this match the framing plan exactly?"
- "Are all shear walls and connectors installed?"
- "Is anything about this unclear before moving forward?"

Chapter 9 Checklist: Framing Readiness

Before moving to rough trades, confirm that you have:

- ☐ Verified wall locations and structural elements
- ☐ Confirmed headers, beams, and shear walls
- ☐ Installed all required hardware
- ☐ Passed framing inspections

☐ Documented framing with photos

Take Action This Week

1. Review framing and shear wall plans in detail.
2. Walk the site daily during framing.
3. Schedule inspections before insulation or rough trades begin.

FINAL TAKEAWAY

Framing is the skeleton of your ADU. When it is built exactly as designed, everything that follows becomes easier, faster, and safer.

CHAPTER 10

ROUGH-INS: ELECTRICAL, PLUMBING, AND HVAC

In ADU projects that fail inspections or require costly rework, the rough-in phase is often where coordination broke down—not craftsmanship.

Once framing is complete, the project moves into the **rough-in stage**. This is when the systems that make your ADU livable—**electrical, plumbing, and heating and cooling (HVAC)**—are installed inside the walls, floors, and ceilings.

After this phase, insulation and drywall will cover everything. At that point, changes become difficult and expensive. That is why planning, sequencing, and inspection readiness during rough ins are essential.

This chapter explains who to hire, how to coordinate the trades, and how to prepare for rough-in inspection with confidence.

Rough-Ins Are Your Last Easy Correction Point. Once walls are closed, mistakes cost time, money, and momentum.

Hiring Licensed MEP Subcontractors

Rough-in work is regulated for a reason—it affects safety, comfort, and long-term reliability.

Electrical, plumbing, and HVAC **work must be performed by licensed professionals**. This is not optional. Cities will not approve unlicensed work, and insurance coverage may be denied if something goes wrong.

When hiring rough-in subcontractors:

- Verify state license and insurance
- Confirm experience with ADUs or small residential projects
- Ask whether they handle permits and inspections for their trade
- Use a written agreement that clearly defines scope and responsibility

Never allow one subcontractor to "cover" another trade.

One Trade, One License. Electrical, plumbing, and HVAC each require their own licensed specialist.

Coordinating the Rough-In Sequence

Rough-ins are not about speed—they are about order.

These trades work in shared spaces, so coordination is critical to avoid conflicts, rework, and inspection failures.

Plumbing Rough-In (Usually First)

Plumbers typically start by installing:

- Water supply lines

- Drain and vent piping
- Connections for showers, sinks, and toilets

This work must be in place before walls are closed and often before other trades can proceed.

Plumbing Sets the Layout. Once pipes are in place, other systems must work around them.

HVAC Rough-In (Usually Second)

Next, the HVAC contractor installs:

- Ductwork
- Vent and return locations
- Equipment connections

Ducts must be routed carefully to avoid conflicts with framing and plumbing.

Electrical Rough-In (Usually Last)

Electricians typically follow, installing:

- Wiring
- Electrical boxes
- Panel connections

Electrical layouts depend on the final placement of plumbing and HVAC components.

Electrical Is Flexible—Up to a Point. Late changes are easier here, but still costly if repeated.

You may need brief return visits if adjustments are required. Clear communication between trades minimizes these disruptions.

Preparing for the Rough-In Inspection

The rough-in inspection is a checkpoint, not a formality.

Before insulation or drywall can begin, the city must inspect all rough-in work.

To prepare:

- Confirm all rough-in work is complete
- Ensure nothing is covered or concealed
- Verify installations match approved plans and Title 24 requirements
- Schedule the inspection in advance

During inspection, the inspector will verify:

- Work was performed by licensed contractors
- Systems meet code requirements
- Safety standards are followed

If something fails inspection, corrections must be completed before moving forward.

Don't Close Walls Early. Covering rough-ins before inspection almost guarantees delays.

Why the Rough-In Phase Is So Important

This phase determines how your ADU will feel to live in.

Rough ins directly affect:

- Comfort and airflow
- Water pressure and drainage
- Electrical capacity and safety

- Energy efficiency and Title 24 compliance

Mistakes here often lead to:

- Costly rework
- Inspection delays
- Reduced comfort or performance

With licensed trades, clear sequencing, and careful inspection preparation, this phase can move smoothly—even for first-time owner-builders.

Scripts & Questions You Can Use

Script for Subcontractors

"We need rough-in work completed and ready for inspection before anything is covered."

Script for Inspectors

"All plumbing, electrical, and HVAC rough ins are complete and ready for inspection."

Questions to Ask

- "Does this match the approved plans and Title 24 report?"
- "Is anything missing before inspection?"
- "Will any future work require reopening walls?"

Rough-In Readiness: Chapter Checklist

Before insulation begins, confirm that you have:

- ☐ Hired licensed electrical, plumbing, and HVAC contractors
- ☐ Completed all rough-in work
- ☐ Coordinated trade sequencing
- ☐ Passed rough-in inspections
- ☐ Documented installations with photos

Take Action This Week

1. Confirm inspection responsibilities with each trade.
2. Walk the site before scheduling inspection.
3. Photograph rough ins for future reference.

FINAL TAKEAWAY

Rough ins are the hidden systems that make your ADU work. When they're installed correctly and inspected properly, everything that follows becomes simpler, cleaner, and more predictable.

CHAPTER 11

DIY FINISH WORK: WALLS, FLOORS, AND TRIM

Across successful owner-built ADUs, finish work is where homeowners most often step in—and where they gain the greatest savings with the least risk.

Once all rough-in inspections are passed, your ADU enters the **finish phase**. This is when the space truly starts to feel like a home. Walls are closed, floors go in, and details like doors and trim bring everything together.

This phase is ideal for hands-on homeowners. The work is more forgiving, tools are easier to use, and mistakes are usually fixable. Taking on finish work yourself can save **thousands of dollars** while giving you full control over the final look of your ADU.

This chapter walks through the main finish tasks step by step, focusing on **where DIY makes sense—and where patience matters most**.

This Is Where Sweat Equity Pays Off. Finish work rewards care and time more than speed or strength.

Insulation and Drywall: Closing the Walls

Once walls are closed, everything inside them is locked in.

Before drywall is installed, insulation must be completed correctly. This step directly affects comfort, energy efficiency, and sound control.

Installing Insulation

Most ADUs use **batt insulation** or **blown-in insulation.**

When installing insulation:

- Follow the R-values specified in your Title 24 report
- Fill wall and ceiling cavities completely
- Do not compress insulation—it reduces effectiveness
- Seal gaps around windows, doors, and penetrations

Insulation Is Performance, Not Appearance. You won't see it later—but you'll feel it every day.

Hanging Drywall

Drywall creates the finished surface for walls and ceilings.

The basic steps include:

- Measuring and cutting sheets to fit
- Securing drywall to framing with screws
- Taping joints and applying joint compound

Drywall is not about speed. Smooth results come from:

- Multiple thin coats
- Proper drying time
- Light sanding between coats

Thin Coats Win. Heavy compound creates more sanding—not better results.

Installing Your Own Flooring

Flooring is one of the most impactful and manageable DIY upgrades. It has a big visual payoff and is forgiving for first-time installers.

Choosing the Right Flooring

Durable, DIY-friendly options include:

- Luxury Vinyl Plank (LVP)
- Laminate
- Engineered wood

These materials are:

- Easy to install
- Cost-effective
- Well-suited for ADUs

Installation Basics

Most floating floors install over underlayment and require:

- A flat, clean subfloor
- Proper expansion gaps at walls
- Careful cuts around doorways and fixtures

Follow the manufacturer's instructions closely—each product is slightly different.

Read the Instructions First. Flooring failures usually come from skipping this step.

Interior Doors and Trim: The Finishing Touches

Doors and trim are what make the space feel intentional.

They hide gaps, define lines, and elevate the overall finish.

Installing Interior Doors

Pre-hung doors are the easiest option for DIY builders.

Focus on:

- Keeping the frame level and plumb
- Using shims to adjust alignment
- Testing the swing before final fastening

If the Door Swings Right, Everything Is Right. Door alignment tells you immediately if something is off.

Baseboards, Casings, and Trim

Trim installation requires precision more than strength.

When installing:

- Measure carefully
- Cut accurately
- Use finish nails or a nail gun
- Fill nail holes and seams before painting

Even simple trim profiles can dramatically improve the finished look.

Why Finish Work Is Perfect for DIY

Finish work is where homeowners gain the most value per hour.

Doing this work yourself allows you to:

- Save significant labor costs
- Work at your own pace
- Customize finishes and details
- Make corrections without major risk

While it requires patience, finish work is where your ADU transforms from a project into a home.

This Is the Creative Phase. Structure and systems are fixed—finishes are where your taste shows.

Scripts You Can Use Immediately

Script for Material Suppliers

"I need materials that are DIY-friendly and compatible with residential ADU use."

Script for Inspectors (If required)

"All insulation meets Title 24 requirements and drywall is ready for final inspection."

Questions to Ask Yourself

- "Does this meet Title 24 requirements?"
- "Am I rushing—or doing it right?"
- "Would fixing this later be harder?"

Finish-Phase Readiness: Chapter Checklist

Before moving to final inspections, confirm that you have:

- ☐ Installed insulation per Title 24
- ☐ Completed drywall and surface prep
- ☐ Installed flooring correctly
- ☐ Hung doors and trim accurately
- ☐ Prepared surfaces for paint

Take Action This Week

1. Choose one finish task you will complete yourself.
2. Gather all tools and materials before starting.
3. Plan extra time—finish quality improves with patience.

FINAL TAKEAWAY

Finish work is where your effort becomes visible. When you slow down and take ownership here, your ADU becomes not just compliant—but personal.

PART IV

PROJECT MANAGEMENT AND FINAL STEPS

CHAPTER 12

SCHEDULING AND ORDERING MATERIALS

In owner-built ADU projects, delays rarely come from hard construction problems—they come from poor timing.

One of the biggest challenges for owner-builders is coordination. If materials arrive too early, they take up space, get damaged, or disappear. If they arrive too late, subcontractors wait, schedules slip, and costs rise.

A clear construction schedule and a simple system for ordering materials keep your ADU moving forward without unnecessary stress.

This chapter explains how to plan a realistic timeline and manage materials efficiently—without complicated software or full-time supervision.

Time Is a Cost. Idle crews and rushed orders quietly drain your budget.

Creating a Simple Construction Schedule

You don't need fancy software—you need clarity.

A workable schedule shows:

- What happens next

- Who is involved
- What must be completed first

For most ADUs, a simple timeline is enough.

A Typical ADU Construction Sequence

Most ADU projects follow this general order:

1. Site preparation and foundation
2. Framing
3. Rough ins (plumbing, electrical, HVAC)
4. Inspections
5. Insulation and drywall
6. Interior finishes
7. Final inspections

Each phase depends on the one before it.

One Phase Unlocks the Next. Skipping steps or rushing inspections always causes setbacks later.

Scheduling Tips for Owner-Builders

To keep your schedule realistic:

- Talk to subcontractors early about availability
- Confirm start dates a few days in advance
- Avoid stacking multiple trades in the same space
- Build in buffer time for:
  - Inspections
  - Weather

- o Minor corrections

A realistic schedule reduces stress—and makes subcontractors more likely to respect your project.

Flexibility Is a Skill. Good schedules absorb delays instead of collapsing under them.

Ordering Materials Without Overbuying or Delaying Work

Material ordering is less about volume and more about timing.

Buying too much too early creates clutter and risk. Buying too late creates delays.

Use Your Plans as a Shopping Guide

Your approved plans, specifications, and reports already tell you most of what you need.

Use them to:

- Avoid guessing
- Match code and Title 24 requirements
- Prevent unnecessary substitutions

Plans Reduce Decision Fatigue. If it's in the plans, you don't need to reinvent it.

Order Materials in Phases

Instead of buying everything at once, order materials by construction phase:

- Foundation phase: concrete-related materials and

hardware

- Framing phase: lumber, connectors, sheathing
- Finish phase: drywall, flooring, doors, trim

This reduces storage issues and limits damage or theft.

Confirm Lead Times Early

Some materials require long lead times, including:

- Windows
- Exterior doors
- Custom fixtures or finishes

Order these early and track delivery dates carefully.

Late Materials Stop Everything. A missing window can delay inspections and stall multiple trades.

Managing Materials on Site

Once materials arrive, organization protects your schedule and your budget.

Storage and Protection

On-site materials should be:

- Kept off the ground
- Covered from weather
- Stored securely when valuable

Damage and theft are more common than most homeowners expect.

Inventory Tracking

When materials arrive:

- Check deliveries immediately
- Compare quantities to invoices
- Note damage or shortages right away

Early documentation prevents disputes and delays.

Inspect Deliveries the Same Day. Waiting even 24 hours can complicate returns or replacements.

Why Scheduling and Materials Matter So Much

Good planning turns chaos into momentum.

Strong scheduling and material management:

- Prevent unnecessary delays
- Reduce wasted money
- Make subcontractors easier to coordinate
- Keep inspections and phases aligned

When you control timing and supplies, you stay in control of the project.

Scripts & Questions You Can Use

Script for Subcontractors

"I'll confirm start dates a few days ahead, so materials and inspections are ready."

Script for Suppliers

"What's the current lead time, and can you confirm delivery in writing?"

Questions to Ask Yourself

- "Does this material arrive before it's needed—or too early?"
- "What happens if this delivery is late?"
- "Do I have space to store this safely?"

Scheduling & Materials Readiness: Chapter Checklist

Before the next phase begins, confirm that you have:

- ☐ A clear construction sequence
- ☐ Start dates coordinated with subcontractors
- ☐ Materials ordered by phase
- ☐ Long-lead items tracked
- ☐ A system for checking deliveries

Take Action This Week

1. Create a one-page construction timeline.
2. List materials needed for the next phase only.
3. Identify any long-lead items that must be ordered now.

FINAL TAKEAWAY

You don't need perfect timing—just intentional timing. When scheduling and materials are managed together, your ADU build becomes predictable instead of reactive.

CHAPTER 13

BUDGETING AND TRACKING OWNER-BUILDER COSTS

In owner-built ADU projects, savings don't come from cutting corners—they come from paying attention. One of the biggest advantages of being an owner-builder is cost control. But that advantage only works if you track your spending carefully. Without a clear budget and a simple system to monitor expenses, small costs quietly add up and erase the savings you worked so hard to create.

This chapter shows you how to build a realistic ADU budget and how to track every dollar so there are no surprises halfway through construction.

What You Don't Track, You Can't Control. Most budget overruns come from untracked "small" expenses.

Creating a Realistic ADU Budget

A good budget is not a guess—it's a decision-making tool.

Start by breaking your project into clear, logical categories. This makes costs easier to understand, track, and adjust.

Typical Owner-Builder ADU Budget Categories

Design and Permits

- Architectural or design fees
- Structural engineering
- Title 24 energy report
- Permit and plan review fees

Site Work and Foundation

- Demolition and grading
- Trenching and utilities
- Concrete and foundation work

Framing

- Lumber and sheathing
- Framing labor
- Hardware and connectors

Mechanical, Electrical, and Plumbing (MEP)

- Plumbing materials and labor
- Electrical materials and labor
- HVAC system and installation

Interior Finishes

- Insulation and drywall

- Flooring
- Doors and trim
- Paint and hardware

Fixtures and Appliances

- Kitchen and bathroom fixtures
- Lighting
- Appliances

Contingency Fund

- 10–15% of the total project budget for unexpected costs

Contingency Is Not "Extra Money". It's protection against surprises—not permission to overspend.

Breaking your budget into categories gives you visibility—and visibility creates control.

Why Tracking Costs Matters So Much

Budgeting sets the plan. Tracking keeps it real.

Tracking expenses in real time allows you to:

- Spot problems early
- Adjust future decisions
- Avoid running out of funds mid-project

Many owner-builders overspend not because prices are unreasonable, but because small purchases go unrecorded.

Small Costs Add Up Quietly. Tools, fasteners, upgrades, and

rush orders are common budget leaks.

Using a Simple Cost-Tracking Spreadsheet

You don't need accounting software—you need consistency.

A basic spreadsheet works extremely well if it's kept current.

Your tracking sheet should include:

- Category (framing, plumbing, finishes, etc.)
- Vendor or subcontractor
- Expense description
- Budgeted amount
- Actual cost
- Date paid
- Notes (change order, upgrade, correction, etc.)

Update your spreadsheet weekly—or after every payment.

Weekly Updates Prevent Monthly Panic. Delayed tracking leads to unpleasant surprises.

Comparing Budget vs. Actual Costs

The most important budgeting habit is comparison.

Regularly compare what you planned to spend versus what you actually spent.

If one category runs over budget:

- Look for savings in another category
- Delay non-essential upgrades
- Use contingency funds intentionally—not automatically

Flexibility Protects the Whole Budget. One overage doesn't mean failure—ignoring it does.

Why This System Works for Owner-Builders

Control beats perfection.

Budgeting and tracking may not feel exciting, but they give you something invaluable: confidence.

When you know where your money is going:

- Decisions become clearer
- Stress goes down
- Trade-offs feel intentional instead of reactive

With a clear budget and a simple tracking system, cost savings turn into real, measurable results.

Scripts You Can Use Immediately

Script for Subcontractors

"Can you break this price into labor and materials so I can track it accurately?"

Script for Suppliers

"Is there a price difference if I order this later or in smaller quantities?"

Questions to Ask Yourself

- "Is this a need—or an upgrade?"

- "If I spend more here, where will I save later?"
- "Does this change affect inspections or only appearance?"

Chapter 13 Checklist: Budget Control

Before the next phase begins, confirm that you have:

- ☐ A complete, categorized budget
- ☐ A contingency fund set aside
- ☐ A cost-tracking spreadsheet in use
- ☐ Updated actual costs weekly
- ☐ Compared budget vs. actual regularly

Take Action This Week

1. Create or finalize your ADU budget categories.
2. Start a simple cost-tracking spreadsheet.
3. Enter every expense—even small ones.

FINAL TAKEAWAY

Budgeting isn't about restriction—it's about awareness. When you track costs consistently, you protect your savings and keep control of your ADU project.

On next page

Category	Description	Estimated Cost ($)
Design & Permits	Architect / Designer	$ 12,000.00
Design & Permits	Structural Engineering	$ 6,000.00
Design & Permits	Title 24 Energy Report	$ 2,500.00
Design & Permits	City Permits & Fees	$ 5,000.00
Site Work	Demolition & Grading	$ 8,000.00
Site Work	Trenching & Utilities	$ 9,000.00
Foundation	Concrete & Foundation	$ 18,000.00
Framing	Lumber & Sheathing	$ 22,000.00
Framing	Framing Labor	$ 18,000.00
MEP	Plumbing	$ 14,000.00
MEP	Electrical	$ 12,000.00
MEP	HVAC	$ 10,000.00
Finishes	Insulation & Drywall	$ 11,000.00
Finishes	Flooring	$ 9,000.00
Finishes	Doors & Trim	$ 7,000.00
Finishes	Paint	$ 6,000.00
Fixtures	Kitchen & Bath Fixtures	$ 10,000.00
Fixtures	Lighting & Appliances	$ 8,000.00
Contingency	10–15% Contingency	$ 20,000.00

CHAPTER 14

INSPECTIONS AND FINAL SIGN-OFF

In successful ADU projects, final inspections are not the most stressful phase—they are the most predictable, because all the real work has already been done.

As construction nears completion, your project enters its final and most important phase: **inspections and approval**. This process confirms that your ADU was built safely, legally, and according to the approved plans. Once complete, the city issues a **Certificate of Occupancy (CO)**, allowing the ADU to be legally used and occupied.

For many owner-builders, inspections feel intimidating. In reality, they are simply a **verification step**—not a test designed to trip you up.

This chapter explains what inspectors look for, how to prepare, and how to move confidently toward final sign-off.

Inspections Confirm Success. They don't undo your work—they validate it.

Understanding the Final Inspection Process

Final inspections close the loop on everything you've built.

Throughout construction, inspections confirmed work at key

stages. Final inspections verify that:

- All work matches the approved plans
- Systems were installed correctly
- Safety and energy codes were met

Inspectors are not there to judge design choices or workmanship style. Their role is to confirm code compliance and safety.

Inspectors Verify—They Don't Design. If it matches the plans and code, it passes.

Preparing for Final Inspections

Preparation turns inspections into a formality.

Before requesting final inspection, confirm that:

- All construction work is complete
- Fixtures, appliances, and finishes are installed
- Required safety devices are in place (smoke and carbon monoxide detectors)
- Title 24 energy requirements are fully met

A clean, organized site also makes inspections faster and smoother.

Finished Means Finished. Missing covers, unfinished trim, or incomplete fixtures often cause delays.

Common Final Inspections You May Need

Some cities combine inspections—others separate them by trade. Your jurisdiction may require one final inspection or several smaller ones.

Building Inspection

Verifies:

- Walls, ceilings, doors, and stairs
- General construction quality
- Safe egress and access

Electrical Inspection

Checks:

- Outlets and lighting
- Panel labeling
- Grounding and safety devices

Plumbing Inspection

Verifies:

- Fixtures and drains
- Water heater installation
- Proper venting and connections

Mechanical (HVAC) Inspection

Confirms:

- Heating and cooling operation
- Venting and airflow
- Energy-efficiency compliance

Energy Compliance Verification

Ensures:

- Installed insulation, windows, lighting, and systems match the Title 24 report

The Inspector Has the Title 24 Report. What's installed must match what was approved.

What Happens If Something Doesn't Pass?

Corrections are normal—and usually minor.

If an inspector notes corrections:

- You will receive a list of items to address
- Corrections are made
- A re-inspection is scheduled

Most final corrections involve:

- Missing labels or covers
- Minor adjustments
- Documentation clarifications

Corrections Are Not Failure. They are part of the final polish—not a setback.

Receiving Your Certificate of Occupancy

This is the document that makes everything official.

Once all final inspections are approved, the city issues a **Certificate of Occupancy (CO)**. This confirms that:

- The ADU meets all building and safety codes
- The unit is legal to occupy or rent

Without a CO, the ADU cannot be legally used, even if construction is complete.

No CO = No Legal Use. The Certificate of Occupancy is the finish line.

Why Final Sign-Off Matters

Final approval protects everything you've built.

It safeguards:

- Your financial investment
- Your ability to rent or house family legally
- Your property value
- Your insurance coverage

Reaching this point means you successfully managed the entire ADU process—from vision and planning through construction and compliance—as an owner-builder.

Scripts You Can Use Immediately

Script for Scheduling Final Inspection

"All work is complete and ready for final inspection and sign-off."

Script for Inspectors

"Everything was built per the approved plans and prior inspection approvals."

Questions to Ask

- "Are there any remaining items before CO issuance?"
- "Is documentation required after approval?"
- "When should I expect the Certificate of Occupancy?"

Final Approval Readiness: Chapter Checklist

Before requesting final sign-off, confirm that you have:

- ☐ Completed all construction work
- ☐ Installed required safety devices
- ☐ Met all Title 24 requirements
- ☐ Passed all final inspections
- ☐ Received your Certificate of Occupancy

Take Action This Week

1. Walk the ADU room by room as if you were the inspector.
2. Test all fixtures, outlets, and systems.
3. Schedule your final inspection with confidence.

FINAL TAKEAWAY

Final inspections are not the end of the journey—they are confirmation that you did it right.

A Milestone Worth Celebrating

Receiving your Certificate of Occupancy is more than paperwork. It is the official completion of your Design-Driven DIY ADU—a safe, legal, fully approved living space built with intention, control, and informed decision-making.

You didn't just build an ADU.

You managed a complex project successfully—and now you get to enjoy the results.

CONCLUSION

THE PERMIT IS NOT THE END, IT'S THE BEGINNING

You have navigated the Great Disconnect between state law and city hall. You assembled an undeniable permit package, survived plan check, managed inspections, and reached the finish line with a Certificate of Occupancy in your hand—a document that is more than approval. It proves you did what most homeowners never do: you finished.

In one of the most challenging regulatory environments in the country, you moved a project from concept to legal reality. And while this may feel like the end of your ADU journey, it is actually the beginning of everything the ADU was meant to deliver.

The permit is the legal foundation beneath every financial and lifestyle benefit your ADU can now provide. It gives you the ability to rent with confidence, house family safely, add real, appraisable value to your property, insure the structure properly, and operate without enforcement risk or future disputes.

What you accomplished goes far beyond construction. You learned how to interpret codes, enforce your rights under state law, manage bureaucracy strategically, and communicate professionally with agencies. You learned how to protect your time, money, and leverage—skills that will serve you in future projects, refinances, negotiations, and property decisions.

With the Certificate of Occupancy issued, the shift is complete. You are no longer asking for permission; you are exercising your rights. Your ADU is now legal, defensible, insurable, and valuable.

The permit maze is behind you. From this point forward, you are no longer navigating bureaucracy—you are managing an asset. One whose income potential, flexibility, security, and long-term value are just beginning, backed by the confidence that comes from knowing the system now works for you.

Made in United States
Troutdale, OR
11/03/2026

56844690R00070